Dryburgh Abbey

James Richardson
and Marguerite Wood

HISTORIC SCOTLAND

'O fear not the priest, who sleepeth to the east!
For to Dryburgh the way he has tae'n;
And there to say mass till three days to pass,
For the soul of a knight that is slayne.

The varying light deceived thy sight,
And the wild winds drown'd the name;
For the Dryburgh bells ring, and the
white monks do sing,
For Sir Richard of Coldinghame!'

(Sir Walter Scott, *The Eve of St John*)

A Guided Tour

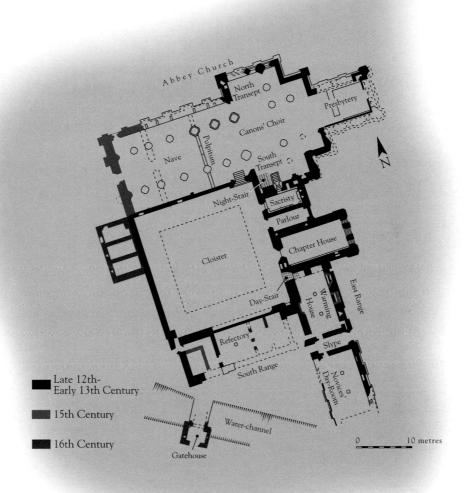

Abbey Church

North Transept

Presbytery

Canons' Choir

Pulpitum

Nave

South Transept

Night-Stair

Sacristy

Parlour

Cloister

Chapter House

Day-Stair

Warming House

East Range

Refectory

Slype

South Range

Novices' Day-Room

Water-channel

Gatehouse

Late 12th-
Early 13th Century

15th Century

16th Century

0   10 metres

N

This tour guides the visitor around the abbey beginning at the west door of the church. To arrive at that point follow the path from the custodian's office along the side of the graveyard. During its life the abbey was divided from the 'toun', or village, of Dryburgh to its north by a precinct wall, described as a 'mantle wall' in 1584, but no trace of this has been found. The first glimpse of the abbey ruins is through the trees. The stone is a clean, crisp, pink sandstone, quarried and carved close by.

The abbey complex covers three terraces which step down southward towards the river. The church sits on the highest terrace, the cloister on the middle terrace with other cloistral buildings below. Although ruined, Dryburgh Abbey rewards the visitor with an insight into medieval monastic life as well as revealing fine examples of ecclesiastic architecture and mason-work.

The Abbey Church

A view through the west door of the church
looking towards the north transept.

The inner face of the west wall of the church, showing one engaged pillar and the remnants of the stone vault over the north aisle of the nave.

The abbey church was dedicated to St Mary the Virgin. On plan it is shaped like a stepped cross. It has a nave, north and south transepts with chapels protruding from their eastern walls, and a rectangular presbytery. A bell tower once rose over the crossing, and we must be thankful that when it collapsed it did not demolish the north transept, which remains the finest hint of what has been lost. Although construction work on the church began in the latter half of the twelfth century, most of what remains dates either to the early thirteenth century or to the rebuilding following the devastation of 1385.

The West Door

The church is entered through the west door which, like the remainder of the west end of the church, dates to the rebuilding after 1385. The door is round-headed, heavily moulded and decorated with blocks, each ornamented with stylised leaves. To either side are buttresses, and beyond them lancet windows. The elevation above the door probably contained a large traceried window (see page 18).

The Nave

So little of the nave remains that any reconstruction would be largely conjecture. However, from the evidence of the junction where the north aisle meets the west wall of the church it is clear that the **aisles flanking the nave** were vaulted over in stone. Each aisle was separated from the central part of the nave by an arcade of six pillars and one engaged pillar on the inner face of the west wall. At the west end of the north wall are the remains of a **doorway**. This would have been the normal entrance into the church for lay folk attending services; the west door would have been used only on high days and holy days.

At the east end of the south wall two *piscinae*, or stone basins, indicate that this area at least was divided into small **chapels** where the canons offered up private prayers for their benefactors. The altar vessels were rinsed in the *piscinae* after the celebration of mass.

One of the piscinae *in the south nave aisle.*

The Merelles Board

The north wall provides an unusual insight into the daily life of the masons who built it. Crudely scratched onto a stone is a board used by the men to play the game of merelles or 'nine men's morris', no doubt during wet lunch-breaks. Very few have been found in Scotland and all are associated with monastic houses. Another fine example is on display at Jedburgh Abbey.

*The remnants of the north (left)
and south (right) transepts.*

The Canons' Choir

The nave at Dryburgh would have been used from the outset by the lay folk of the district for worship. It was closed off from the canons' own choir by a *pulpitum*, or stone screen, placed across the fourth pair of pillars reading from the west. The foundations alone remain with the threshold of its doorway in the centre. To its east lay the canons' choir, the heart of the abbey (see the reconstruction drawing on page 25). Their choir-stalls stretched from the *pulpitum* eastward across the central crossing and beneath the bell tower to the presbytery at the east end. The brethren spent the greater part of their day in the church and their stalls would doubtless have been beautifully carved and of the highest quality to reflect the importance attached to this part of the church.

The Transepts

The north transept chapels looking north.

To north and south of the central crossing were the transepts, or cross-arms, each projecting a bay's width beyond the nave aisles. These provided additional space, chiefly for chapels for private devotion. The transepts had steep-pitched timber roofs, whilst the chapels projecting from the east were vaulted over in stone.

The **north transept** is the more complete and much of the carving is as crisp as the day it was done. The north gable, now largely gone, had two tiers of three lancets, each similarly decorated inside and out; the elevations around the west and south sides of the chapels are of an elegant three-storeyed design. Above the pointed arches leading into the chapels is a shallow triforium, or gallery, decorated with circular openings within arched recesses. At the top is a taller clearstory with pointed arches fronting a wall-passage. The architecture shows signs of having been modified as work progressed ~ for example, the clearstory arcade next to the presbytery has five arches whereas the others have only three - and the circular openings also appear to have been altered. Behind these openings was a storage space reached from the clearstory, which in turn was reached by a spiral stair in the north-west corner of the transept.

The two eastern **chapels** differ in size, the inner one two bays deep with arches opening into the presbytery and the outer chapel one bay deep with an arch opening into the transept. The fixing holes for the wooden screens enclosing each chapel are visible cut into the masonry. The chapel vaults have moulded ribs and great carved keystones, or bosses, holding them together. One boss (see left) depicts Christ in Majesty with one hand raised to bless His flock and with a book clasped in the other.

Each chapel housed an altar; the *piscina* serving the altar in the north chapel still survives. When the abbey was abandoned by the canons, these chapels were appropriated for private burial-places by notable families of the district, among them the Haliburtons and the Haigs of Bemersyde. Their most distinguished representatives, Sir Walter Scott and Earl Haig, are buried there (see page 34).

The **south transept** mirrored the arrangement in the north transept but only the splendid south gable remains. This has a magnificent window composed of five lancets, stepped at their bases to accommodate the roof of the dormitory on the outside.

The tombstone of John Haliburton (died 1640) in the north transept. John Haliburton was an ancestor of Sir Walter Scott, who is interred nearby.

The **night-stair**, used by the canons when going to and from their night-time services, passes through the large round-headed doorway in the west side of the gable. The smaller, lintelled doorway to its east led to what was the sacristy, but was modified when the sacristy became a private burial aisle. In the south-east corner of the transept is a small round-headed door which led down to the vestry but which also gave access to a spiral stair from which the dormitory, the clearstory and the bell-chamber were reached.

The Presbytery

The presbytery at the east end of the church, beyond the canons' choir, housed the high altar. Like the nave, it is now so ruinous that it belies accurate description. On the evidence of the surviving north wall, the north and south walls probably each had three lancets. The east wall probably continued the theme. Below the windows the wall stepped in slightly to take an arcade of engaged, intersecting arches supported on short pillars, similar to those in the east wall of the chapter house.

The high altar was probably originally placed against this east wall but seems to have been relocated a little further west against a screen, the stone footings of which remain. The space behind the screen may have been a chapel, perhaps housing a reliquary cherished by the canons.

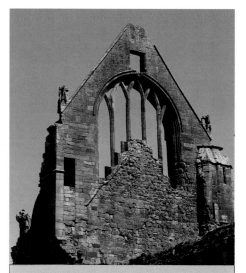

The great vertical window in the south transept gable that brought light into the church.

Main photograph: The east end of the church from the north-east, and (inset) a detail of the interior of one of the chapels with a piscina *below the springing of the vault ribs.*

Church

Cloister

Chapter
house

Day-stair

Warm
room

Refectory

The Cloister Buildings

As was usual in monastic planning, the domestic accommodation was placed around a cloister on the south side of the church so that the great height of the church did not block out the light. The canons' home lay in two ranges built along the east and south sides of the cloister, and at Dryburgh these are unusually complete and informative. The east range housed the most important rooms, including the chapter house, the warming room and the novices' day room; the south range housed the refectory and kitchen. The west side of the cloister does not appear to have had a range, just an enclosing wall.

Around the four sides of the cloister garden was a covered walk, which sheltered the brethren from the elements as they moved about the monastery. The roof along the east cloister walk was originally carried on a stone vault but this was later removed and replaced by a timber framework largely carried on projecting stone corbels. On the outer edge the sloping roof would have been supported on an open arcade, giving the canons views into the cloister garden. The covered walk was also used for private study, as the shelved book-cupboard (see below) in the east wall beside the processional door confirms.

The tour begins in the dormitory on the upper floor of the east range because this may only be reached directly from the church. The remainder of the complex is reached through the east processional door.

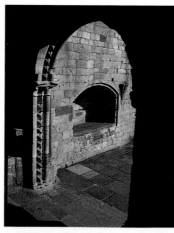

Dormitory

Slype

Novices' day room

The cloister as it might have looked before the English raid of 1385.

The Dormitory

and Commendator's House

A bat peers down on all who pass up the night-stair from church to dormitory.

The fine arched head of the east processional door.

The dormitory, or dorter, was at the head of the night-stair, lit from the west by a transept window with a quaint carving of a small bat in its left side, a nice touch of humour by one of the masons. The dormitory originally ran the whole length of the east range but was probably divided into individual cells by timber partitions.

The east cloister range as it might have looked when altered to form a house for the commendators.

Halfway along the room was the **day-stair** leading down to the cloister. Perhaps this stair marked the division between the sleeping accommodation reserved for the canons, who would have been nearer the church, and that of the novices. Beyond the novices' quarters, at the south end of the range, would have been the **latrine-block**, or reredorter, in which position it could be flushed by the main water-channel.

The dormitory has undergone several changes during its life. The original roof line is visible in the north wall, below the five-light window, but this seems to have been destroyed by fire, judging by the heat-cracked stones in the transept gable. Unusually, the replacement roof seems to have been raised to the full height of the gable to provide additional accommodation. The double tier of windows and the blocked up south transept window are clearly

shown on Slezer's engraving dated 1678 (see page 29).

The final change was carried out in the later sixteenth century to provide a **private house** for the commendator of the abbey. This was built in the north end of the former dormitory, above the chapter house and parlour, and consisted of a two-storeyed house with a north wing. The house was entered from a fore-stair placed against the east, or outer, side of the east range.

The Processional Door

The cloister is reached through the east processional door in the south aisle of the church. This is the only door still in use of three that linked the church to the cloister. It was actually removed to the mansion of Newton Don, near Kelso, but was reinstated in 1894. The grandeur of the door emphasises not only the importance of the church but also of the cloister as part of the processional route taken by the brethren during important services. The round-headed door is moulded and ornamented with dog-tooth decoration and the splayed sides have recessed orders with disengaged shafts. The caps for these shafts are plain on the east side and decorated with water-leaf designs on the west.

The dormitory and south transept gable looking north, with the east processional door to the left. The raggle of the original roof of the dormitory is visible immediately below the great window. After 1322, the east range was given an extra floor and the roof raised to the full height of the gable (see the engraving on page 29).

The East Range

The first room reached along the east range may once have been divided by a timber partition into two rooms, one a **library** and the other a **sacristy** where items used in the church (for example, altar frontals and vestments) were stored and where the celebrants at mass robed (see the reconstruction drawing on page 25). This barrel-vaulted chamber, now known as St Modan's Chapel after the Celtic missionary associated with Dryburgh, also had two exits into the south transept of the church. It was originally lit by two windows in the east wall, but at some later date an almond-shaped window was inserted above them. The room has stone benches around the walls. It became the Buchan burial aisle after the eleventh earl purchased Dryburgh in 1786 and is not normally accessible (see page 32).

The cloister walk along the east range ran between these two round-headed doorways.

The **parlour** next to the sacristy served both as a passageway to the burial-ground beyond the east range and as a meeting place where the canons, otherwise bound to a vow of silence, were permitted necessary conversation. The space may have had timber benches along the side walls and originally had doors at either end, but when it became a private burial vault in the nineteenth century the eastern opening was built up and a window inserted.

The east cloister walk looking towards the church with the entrances to the sacristy, the parlour and the chapter house.

Main photograph: The interior of the chapter house. The importance of this business room is emphasised by the superb entrance, with its finely-decorated doorway (above and right).

The Chapter House

The chapter house is entered through a splendid round-headed door with similar decoration to the east processional door. It is flanked by twin-light windows in late twelfth-century style. Down a modern flight of steps is the chapter house itself. The status of the room is obvious from the grand entrance and its size; it stretches beyond all the other chambers in the east range. Second only in importance to the church, the chapter house was where the business of the abbey was conducted, tasks handed out, sins confessed and discipline applied.

The canons sat on the stone seats around the walls. The more elaborate arcaded seating along the east wall was clearly reserved for the abbot and his senior office-bearers. Each stone arch had a painted geometric pattern in the upper part and a hanging below. The arches dividing the seats along the side walls were achieved with paint rather than costly stone work. Coloured painting-work is visible elsewhere in the chapter house; for example, the white-plastered wall surfaces were painted with imitation jointing in red, and chevrons and other patterns remain in isolated places such as around the north window.

The chapter house from the monastic burial ground to the east. The importance of the chapter house is further emphasised by the way the building extends beyond the rest of the east range.

The chapter house as it might have looked in the fourteenth century. Traces of the brightly-coloured decoration can be seen between the intersecting arches of the office-bearers' seats on the east wall (above left), on the moulding at the springing of the vault (above right) and on the outer edges of the window arches. The vaulted ceiling was white plastered and lined out in red ~ making it look for all the world like a station on the London Underground!

The Warming House

and Novices' Day Room

In the south-east corner the cloister **stair** leads down from the middle terrace to the lowest terrace and the other rooms in the east range. The door at the top of the stair was secured by a timber draw-bar, the slot for which is visible in the west side.

The warming house, or calefactory, was the one place where the canons were allowed the comfort of a fire. It was once ceiled with an elegant rib-vault carried on central pillars and slender corbels. In the fourteenth century the windows were enlarged to their present appearance and the fireplace moved from the east to the west wall. The new hooded **fireplace** has corbels decorated with oak leaves and acorns. A wall-closet opens from the south-east corner of the room.

Across a short barrel-vaulted **passage**, or slype, from the warming house is a chamber identified as the **novices' day room**, where new members received instruction from the novice master. The room resembles the earlier warming house with the fireplace in the east wall and the original window form.

The warming house looking south, showing many signs of change. The two large windows on the ground floor were inserted in the fourteenth century, causing the original fireplace which used to be there to be moved to the opposite wall. The thickening of the wall on the floor above was necessitated by the rebuilding of the upper levels as the result of fire damage.

The South Range
and Gatehouse

The south range was dedicated to the basic requirements of food and drink. The basement **undercrofts** were originally rib-vaulted but in the fifteenth century barrel vaults were inserted and a passage created towards the west end. The vaults provided storage for food and wine. Over them was the **dining hall**, or refectory, little of which survives. It was entered from the south cloister walk. The arched recess in the south-west corner of the cloister was probably the **wash-place**, or lavatory, where the canons washed their hands before sitting down to table. The lead-lined trough and lead piping have disappeared and the present stone bench and back are restoration features.

The refectory would have been well lit by windows in the north and south walls but only the splendid rose-window high up in the west gable survives (see the photograph on page 28). This is almost identical to the fifteenth-century rose-window in Jedburgh Abbey church. Beneath the window and divided from the refectory by a screen was the servery from the **kitchen**, housed in a separate building beyond the west wall. The high table would have been at the east end with a pulpit close by from which one of the brethren would read each day from the Bible or an uplifting tome, ensuring that the canons' minds received sustenance as well as their stomachs. Below the servery was a passage from the cloister to the kitchen. The doorway from the cloister has the arms of John Stewart (see page 30), son of the earl of Lennox, and a commendator of the abbey, and below it a stone incised with B (for Buchan) and the date 1788.

To the south of the cloistral buildings was the main **water-channel** filled with water drawn from the river. A **bridge** was built over it and a **gatehouse** beyond. The gatehouse, dating to the sixteenth century, has the arms of the Greenlaw and Ker families on heraldic shields carved on the skew-putts. In the parkland beyond is a stone **obelisk** (see page 21) erected by the earl of Buchan in 1794.

Above: the abbey from the south. Below: the south range and gatehouse viewed from along the water-channel, now flowing with flowers rather than water. The scene is dominated by the attractive rose-window that lit the monks refectory beyond.

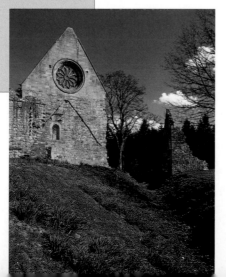

The Story of the Abbey

Dryburgh Abbey was regarded as a peaceful refuge for those weary of this world and anxious to prepare for the next. Peaceful it may have been, and secluded, but it could not escape altogether from the conflict of the secular world, either in the land-courts or from passing armies.

St Modan the Missionary

The quiet seclusion of Dryburgh is the perfect setting for the home of an early Christian missionary and therefore it is no surprise to read in a medieval *Calendar of Scottish Saints* that this enchanting spot is associated with St Modan. Like many figures from the Dark Ages, Modan's life is shrouded in mystery. He is thought to have lived in the late sixth and early seventh century and hailed from Argyll. A follower of St Columba, he began his missionary work around Loch Etive before moving east and south. He is linked with Falkirk and Rosneath, in Dunbartonshire, as well as Dryburgh. Sadly, there is nothing tangible from Dryburgh - no early Christian stones or other artefacts - nor any evidence of an early church to support this literary information.

De Moreville's Foundation

Dryburgh Abbey was founded during a tidal wave of generous piety which began with Malcolm III and Margaret, his queen, in the late eleventh century and reached its peak during the reign of their sixth and youngest son, David I (1124-53). Through the munificence of David and his associates, the majority of Scotland's abbeys and priories were established. Dryburgh was among them.

The obelisk to the south of the abbey set up by the eleventh earl of Buchan to mark the foundation of the abbey in 1150 by Hugh de Moreville.

The abbey was founded in 1150 by Hugh de Moreville, an Anglo-Norman who had befriended David in England and had come north at his invitation. He was granted extensive estates in the eastern Border country ~ chiefly Lauderdale but also along the Tweed at places like Newton Don and Dryburgh ~ as well as the whole of Cunningham, the northern part of Ayrshire. He also held land at Bozeat, in Northamptonshire, in King David's English Honour of Huntingdon, and his marriage to Beatrice de Beauchamp linked him with the greatest landowner in Bedfordshire. By 1150 Hugh was constable of Scotland and one of the most powerful men in the country.

The founding of a religious house would have been a perfectly acceptable thing for Hugh de Moreville to do. Though achieved at great personal cost, it fulfilled two needs; it demonstrated Hugh's standing in society, and it allowed for a perpetual round of prayers to be offered up to God for his soul and those of his family. Hugh was evidently committed to his foundation for in his old age he enrolled as a novice there. He died within its walls in 1162. It is not known if Beatrice, his widow, lived long enough to learn of their son, Hugh's, involvement in the murder of Archbishop Thomas Becket in Canterbury Cathedral in 1170.

The assassination of Thomas Becket in Canterbury Cathedral. Among the four assassins was Hugh de Moreville, son of the founder of Dryburgh Abbey.

The Premonstratensians

Hugh de Moreville invited the Premonstratensians from Alnwick, in Northumberland, to set up the house, their first in Scotland. At that date Prince Henry, King David's son, was earl of Northumbria.

A Premonstratensian canon, taken from a seventeenth-century drawing and showing him wearing his canonical vestments and a fur stole.

The order was relatively recent, established about 1120 by St Norbert. Norbert, a cleric at the court of the archbishop of Cologne, had shown little enthusiasm for the religious life until he was thrown from his horse in a thunderstorm. He retired to a Benedictine abbey where he earned the displeasure of his superiors by attempting reforms. He left, sold all his possessions and began an evangelising mission which laid great stress on personal hardship. After an unpromising start, he eventually found a friend in the bishop of Laon, in northern France, who shared his desire for monastic reform. Norbert was allowed to settle in a ruined Benedictine chapel to the west of Laon, at Premontré, whence the name of the order. He initially adopted the rule of St Augustine, which combined the cloistered life of the monk with the preaching role of the priest. But unhappy with the Augustinians' lack of stress on austerity and personal hardship, he modified it, following closely the Cistercian way of life.

The Premonstratensians were not monks but regular canons, that is priests who lived together in community and followed a *regula* or rule. They were more usually known as 'white canons', from the colour of their habits, and to distinguish them from the Augustinian or 'black' canons. Their first house in England was at Newhouse, in Lincolnshire, in 1143. Alnwick was founded from there in 1147. Dryburgh, a daughter-house of Alnwick, became the premier house of the order in Scotland, although this role was disputed

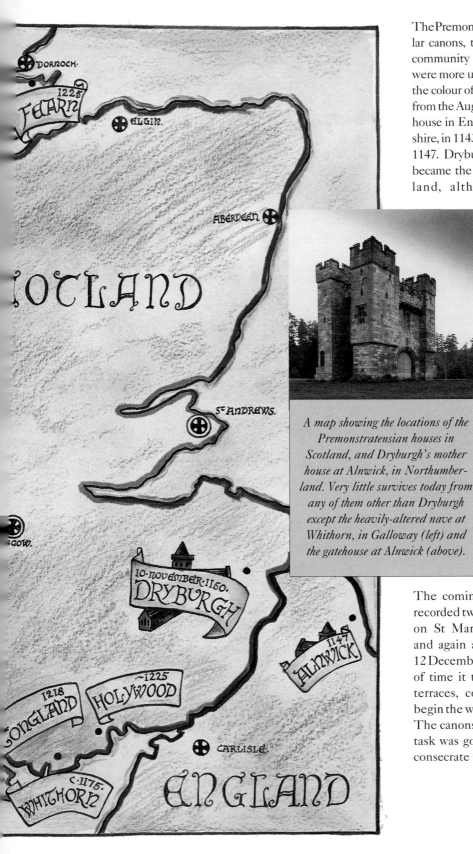

by Soulseat, in Galloway, founded about 1161 direct from Premontré. Four more Scottish Premonstratensian houses were built, none of them founded from Dryburgh. Whithorn (c.1175) and Holywood (or Dercongal, by 1225), both in Galloway, were settled from Soulseat, Tongland (1218), also in Galloway, was settled from Cockersand, in Lancashire, and Fearn (c.1225), in Ross, from Whithorn. Dryburgh, though, had two daughter houses in Ireland, both in County Antrim. Carrickfergus was founded before 1183 and Drumcross by 1250. Both, ironically, suffered severely during the Scottish attack on Ulster in 1315-7 from which Carrickfergus never recovered.

A map showing the locations of the Premonstratensian houses in Scotland, and Dryburgh's mother house at Alnwick, in Northumberland. Very little survives today from any of them other than Dryburgh except the heavily-altered nave at Whithorn, in Galloway (left) and the gatehouse at Alnwick (above).

The coming of the canons to Dryburgh is recorded twice in the *Chronicle of Melrose*, firstly on St Martin's Day (10 November) 1150 and again almost exactly two years later on 12 December 1152. This may reflect the length of time it took to clear the site, lay out the terraces, construct temporary quarters and begin the work of building the church in stone. The canons must have known how hard their task was going to be for their first act was to consecrate the cemetery.

The Daily Round

The whole purpose of an abbey like Dryburgh was to 'create a beacon of prayer in a sinful world'. Much of medieval society depended on the fear of God and the after-life and these 'beacons of prayer' were a kind of passport from this world to the next. The canons in their cloister were expected to offer up a perpetual round of prayers on behalf of those who chose to remain in the outside world, most importantly of course for the founder and his family and others who endowed it.

To this end the canons spent most of their time in the abbey church. They were awakened about one o' clock in the morning by the dormitory bell, rung for as long as it takes to say the seven penitential psalms, and retired about eight o' clock in the evening. In between times, they attended the eight set offices, known as 'hours', celebrated mass and offered up private prayers. When not in church they worked in the cloister, writing, reading and contemplating. Each morning after Prime, the second office of the day, they gathered in the chapter house to discuss the business of the abbey. Twice a day they went to the refectory for frugal, vegetarian meals.

The numbers of canons at any one time is unlikely to have been many more than 20. The organisation of the abbey was under the direction of the abbot and his deputy, the prior. Other office-bearers included the precentor and sacrist, who together were in charge of the church, the novice master, who instructed new recruits, the infirmarer, who oversaw the sick and old, the almoner, who dispensed charity to the poor and needy, and the cellarer, who looked after the provisioning of the abbey.

North transept

Canons' choir

Presbytery

South transept

Sacristy and Library

Cloister walk

25

The Early Years

What little is known of Dryburgh's story comes mainly from the cartulary, or register book, of the abbey. Since this concentrates on the business of the abbey it is not surprising that our impression is of a community accumulating lands and quarrelling over them with the intensity worthy of a better cause. Hugh de Moreville and Beatrice, his wife, were the largest benefactors, liberally bestowing churches and lands from their extensive estates on the order, in England as well as Scotland. In the event, the problem of administering the church at Bozeat from such a distance proved too much and in 1190 the abbey arranged to exchange it for lands in Lauderdale which Helen de Moreville, Hugh's niece, had granted to the abbey of St James in Northampton. Gifts came also from the king, including the church in Lanark, and from other great landowners, like the de Vauxs of Dirleton, in East Lothian, who gave the island of Fidra to the canons in 1220.

Smailholm Church, a little to the east of Dryburgh, was one of numerous parish churches gifted to the abbey.

A beautifully-carved stone basin on display in the abbey. It was found in the west range and may have been used in the wash-place, or lavatory, for the ritual washing of hands, or indeed even the ceremonial washing of hair.

The canons were permitted to serve as priests in the churches they were given but more usually they appointed vicars, or deputies, who were paid a small stipend. The lands were farmed by tenants and the rents collected regularly. It was a system that was bound to involve the white canons in legal dispute, despite their best intentions to lead a quiet and godly life. The earliest recorded dispute, settled in 1177, concerned their holding at Lessuden (now St Boswells), which was contested by the Augustinians from nearby Jedburgh Abbey.

We know little more than the names of the abbots of Dryburgh and less still of the canons. None of the abbots was particularly outstanding either as scholar or as cleric. But in common with all other abbots they held the position of a substantial land-owning lord. The only name of note is Adam, 'an exemplary religious' and an excellent preacher, who succeeded as third abbot some time in the late 1180s. However, while on a visit to Premontré he fell in love with the Carthusian way of life and on his return to Britain he entered the charterhouse at Witham, in Somerset, where he ended his days. Nevertheless his reputation as a preacher and writer was made at Dryburgh. Of the canons, one name stands out, but for the wrong reason. Brother Marcus, we read, was suspended in 1320 for knocking down the abbot with his fist!

The entrance facade of the chapter house, the finest part of the early building to survive.

During these first 100 years or so, Dryburgh would have been anything but quiet and secluded for the work of constructing the great abbey church and of replacing the temporary quarters of the canons with more permanent ranges of buildings would have proceeded apace. Of all this activity the abbey cartulary is silent and we have only the buildings themselves to hint at the progress of the work. The masons would have started first on the east end of the church so that the high altar was made available to the canons at the earliest opportunity. Sadly, very little survives of this part of the church.

The oldest parts of the abbey buildings to survive are within the east range (above) and are characterised by small, round-headed windows (left).

Construction work then seems to have concentrated on the lower walls of the south transept and the east range of the cloister; the east processional door and the chapter house entrance are beautiful examples of late-twelfth-century architecture. The masons then returned to the church to complete the canons' choir; the north transept chapels and the south transept gable are in elegant early thirteenth-century style.

War and Peace

The comparative peace of Dryburgh was shattered during the Wars of Independence with England which erupted in 1296. In 1322 Edward II's army, retreating south after yet another unsuccessful invasion and hearing in the distance the abbey's bells ringing out in celebration, turned aside and set fire to the place. The heat-cracked masonry on the south side of the south transept below the original roof line of the canons' dormitory may be a legacy from this attack, the first of several that afflicted the brethren throughout the later Middle Ages.

The task of rebuilding began almost immediately. King Robert the Bruce gave financial help and Bishop John of Glasgow, in 1326, granted the abbey the church at Maxton as 'an act of piety to succour the needy'. Evidently even this proved insufficient for in 1330 Patrick, a canon of the house, recorded the catastrophe in a poem addressed to the king and the superiors of other religious houses - evidently an appeal for more funds.

The rose window in the west gable of the refectory and (inset) the north wall of the dormitory showing the heat-cracked stone from the 1322 fire.

The Y-shaped traceried windows in the warming house, inserted during the fourteenth century to increase the light.

The west front of the church, rebuilt in the early fifteenth century. The builders chose a round-headed arrangement for the door, perhaps in a conscious effort to recreate the original fine architecture of the abbey.

This engraving by John Slezer of the abbey in the late seventeenth century provides vital evidence for the raising of the east range to the full height of the south transept.

If we associate the clear evidence for the burning down of the dormitory with the events of 1322, then Brother Patrick's appeal was evidently very successful for the reconstruction of the dormitory was on the grand scale, quite unparalleled anywhere else in Scotland. Judging by the evidence in Slezer's engraving of 1678, the canons' new sleeping quarters rose to the full height of the south transept, giving them at least one extra floor. The abandonment of the stone vault over the east cloister walk and its replacement by a timber lean-to roof, and the alterations to the warming house may also have been necessitated by this first recorded English attack.

A period of comparative peace followed and the canons returned to their daily round of prayer. But the ravages of war returned to the cloister in 1385 during Richard II's invasion. The abbey was 'devastated by hostile fire', apparently almost beyond recovery. Robert III, like his namesake and predecessor, gave financial assistance to the abbey in its work of rebuilding. This included the revenues of the Cistercian nunnery in Berwick-upon-Tweed, founded by David I in the twelfth century but now closed because of the dissolute way of life of the ladies therein. Gifts to the abbey by others about this time may also be linked to this work. They included donations from the earl of Douglas, Lord Halyburton of Dirleton and Lord Maxwell of Caerlaverock, in Dumfriesshire.

The rebuilding work is most evident at the west end of the church, particularly the attractive west door. The job must have gone on for many years because as late as 1425 an 'Instrument of perambulation of the marches betwixt Ridpeth and Beymersyde' mentions a yett, or gate, which was used to guard the route for ' the carrying thereby of tymber for the building of the abbacie of Dryburgh'.

The crucifixion of St Andrew depicted on a late-medieval vaulting boss.

The Closing Years

Somehow monastic life continued despite these interruptions, but signs that the austere life of the founding brethren was gradually being eroded had appeared as early as the mid fourteenth century when the abbot received special powers from Rome to deal with indiscipline. Throughout the fifteenth century the canons appeared more intent on defending their earthly treasures in the land-courts than attending to their heavenly goals. In this the Premonstratensians were not alone and by the outset of the sixteenth century the increasingly lax life of the monasteries was leading to calls for reform.

One scandal was the misuse of church appointments. Commendators were originally appointed to levy the fruits of a benefice during a vacancy but during the reigns of James IV (1488-1513) and James V (1513-42) the system was abused, chiefly to reward illegitimate offspring. When Abbot Andrew died in 1507, he was not replaced by another canon, despite the pleas of Dryburgh's chapter who petitioned the king to prefer David Finlayson, their colleague and parish priest in Gullane. Instead, the king nominated James Stewart, illegitimate son of Master John Stewart, though it seems he never took up the appointment. In 1509, the first incumbent as commendator, Andrew Forman, a noted diplomat and ecclesiastic, took up the appointment, though he would scarcely have visited the abbey, his tenure limited to drawing his income. The task of running the abbey now fell to the prior.

Shortly after the death in 1522 of the then commendator, David Hamilton, bishop of Argyll and half-brother of the earl of Arran, war returned to the Borders. The effects on Dryburgh are not recorded but Regent Albany's appeal to the Cardinal Protector of Scotland urging the appointment of a superior who could give his whole attention to the affairs of the house and the repair of the abbey suggests that the canons did not escape the earl of Surrey's raids. The manner in which the appointment was carried out is a good insight into ecclesiastical patronage at this time. Dryburgh was bestowed on a minor, John Stewart, second son of the earl of Lennox, but they in turn transferred the commendatorship to James Stewart, a kinsman and a canon of Glasgow, on condition that he pay the earl's son a generous pension. Quite how this squared with the reason for the appointment, namely the repair of the abbey, is not clear but building work does seem to have been carried out as John Stewart's coat of arms in the south range shows.

The coat of arms of John Stewart, son of the earl of Lennox, above the door at the south-west corner of the cloister.

Dryburgh Abbey and the River Tweed in the late seventeenth century; an engraving by John Slezer.

John Erskine, earl of Mar and guardian to James VI, was a commendator of Dryburgh in the 1560s.

James Stewart died in 1541 and was succeeded by Thomas Erskine, second son of Lord Erskine, to whose family the abbey belonged thereafter. But the end was fast approaching for the canons. In 1544 they were once more devastated by war, this time at the hands of the earl of Hertford's men. The final blow was dealt on 4 November when an English raiding party some 700 strong 'rode into Scotland upon the water of Tweide to a town called Dryburgh with an abbey in the same, which was a pretty town and well buylded; and they burnte the same town and abbey, saving the churche, ... and they tarried so long at the said burnynge and spoylage that it was Satterday at eight of the cloke at nycht or they come home'. Neither the abbey nor the town recovered from the shock.

The Reformation in 1560 spelt the end for monastic life at Dryburgh. Although the commendator, David Erskine, the sub-prior and the eight remaining canons embraced the reformed religion, and by so doing were allowed to remain, no new members were permitted. By now the cloister buildings must have been in an advanced state of decay and the new buildings erected in this period ~ the commendator's house in the shell of the dormitory, the vaulted range against the outside of the west cloister wall and the gatehouse beside the water-channel ~ may reflect the scattered nature of monastic life at this date, the canons leading largely separate lives in their individual plots. In 1580 their numbers were down to four and in 1584 to two. In 1600 a document signed by the commendator included the significant observation that 'all the convent thairof [are] now deceissit'.

Buchan's Romantic Ruin

In 1786, the abbey was purchased by David Steuart Erskine, eleventh earl of Buchan, and a descendant of the Erskines, commendators of Dryburgh. Buchan was a man of ideas and had been the moving spirit behind the foundation of the Society of Antiquaries of Scotland in 1780. He spent a great deal of time and money recording the religious houses of Scotland and researching their origins. He was also a member of the movement which advocated the right of ruins to remain as elegant reminders of our glorious past. During the 40 years he spent at nearby Dryburgh House he created a magnificent garden, planted specimen trees and built classical follies. He also preserved the ruins of the great abbey, making it the most magnificent of garden ornaments. He planted shrubs in the cloister, where he also erected 'a statue of Inigo Jones in the centre of the quadrangle which will have a fine effect in one of the views'.

The grave of David Steuart Erskine, eleventh earl of Buchan, in the former sacristy.

Though a man of consummate taste, Buchan, like most antiquarians of his time, was unable to resist the temptation to meddle and the abbey ruins are full of oddities attributable to him. These include the foundation date ~ 1150 - inscribed on the slype doorway in the east range, the inscription ~ *Hic jacet Archibald* ~ cut into the wall beside the chapter house entrance, and the re-erected grave-slabs around the walls of the presbytery. Most curious of all is his obelisk to the south of the gatehouse (see page 21). Buchan also undertook excavations, and on finding a stone coffin he opened it and removed a chalice (with the finger bones of the poor occupant still attached), the crook and part of the silk shroud. Despite this, it is largely thanks to him that so much remains to enchant us. At his death in 1829, his body was laid to rest in the former sacristy, which he had appropriated as the family burial-vault.

Buchan (inset top) left his mark on Dryburgh Abbey in several ways. The great garden he created in the cloister, illustrated here in Lizar's engraving, has now gone, along with the statue of Inigo Jones. More enduring is the inscription cut into the stone below a window in the chapter house (inset bottom). The drawing of the west door framing the north transept was commissioned by the earl.

CLOISTER
GATE OF THE CHURCH OF ST MARY
DRYBURGH ABBEY.

Sir Walter Scott and Earl Haig

The grave of Field-Marshal Earl Haig of Bemersyde in the north transept.

Two more great men lie entombed within the abbey, Sir Walter Scott of Abbotsford and Field-Marshal Earl Haig of Bemersyde. Both graves are in the north transept chapels, which had been appropriated by their respective families after the Reformation.

It is ironic that Buchan and Scott should reside across the canons' choir from each other for Buchan had had the misfortune in his dotage to be villified by Sir Walter Scott, who succeeded in ruining his reputation. The 'wizard of the North' was buried at Dryburgh by right of his ancestors, the Haliburtons of Newmains; Robert Haliburton, grand-uncle to Sir Walter Scott, had sold the abbey following his bankruptcy. Scott himself wrote: 'we have nothing left of Dryburgh, although my father's paternal inheritance, but the right of stretching our bones where mine may perhaps be laid ere any eye but my own glances over these pages'. Sir Walter was laid to rest in what he called St Mary's Aisle, his 'domus ultimus', on 26 September 1832.

Field-Marshal Earl Haig, who was buried close by Scott in 1928, was commander-in-chief of the British Expeditionary Forces in France and Flanders during World War I. After the war he was granted the title of first earl of Bemersyde in memory of his ancestors, the Haigs, who originated from the district of La Hague in Normandy, had crossed to England in 1066 and who settled at Bemersyde, a little up the hill from Dryburgh, as vassals of Hugh de Moreville, the founder of the abbey. And so our story comes full circle.

The north transept chapels, where Scott and Haig now lie.

A drawing by Captain James Alexander of the funeral procession of Sir Walter Scott arriving at Dryburgh Abbey on 26 September 1832. (Courtesy of Mrs. Patricia Maxwell-Scott of Abbotsford.)

FURTHER READING

I Cowan and D Easson
Medieval Religious Houses: Scotland
(1976)
S Cruden
Scottish Medieval Churches (1986)
R. Fawcett
Scottish Medieval Churches (1985)
R Fawcett
Scottish Abbeys and Priories (1994)
K Stringer
'Dryburgh Abbey and Bozeat,
Northamptonshire', *Innes Review*,
vol 24, ii (1973)